A PARTNERSHIP AGENDA FOR FISHERIES CONSERVATION

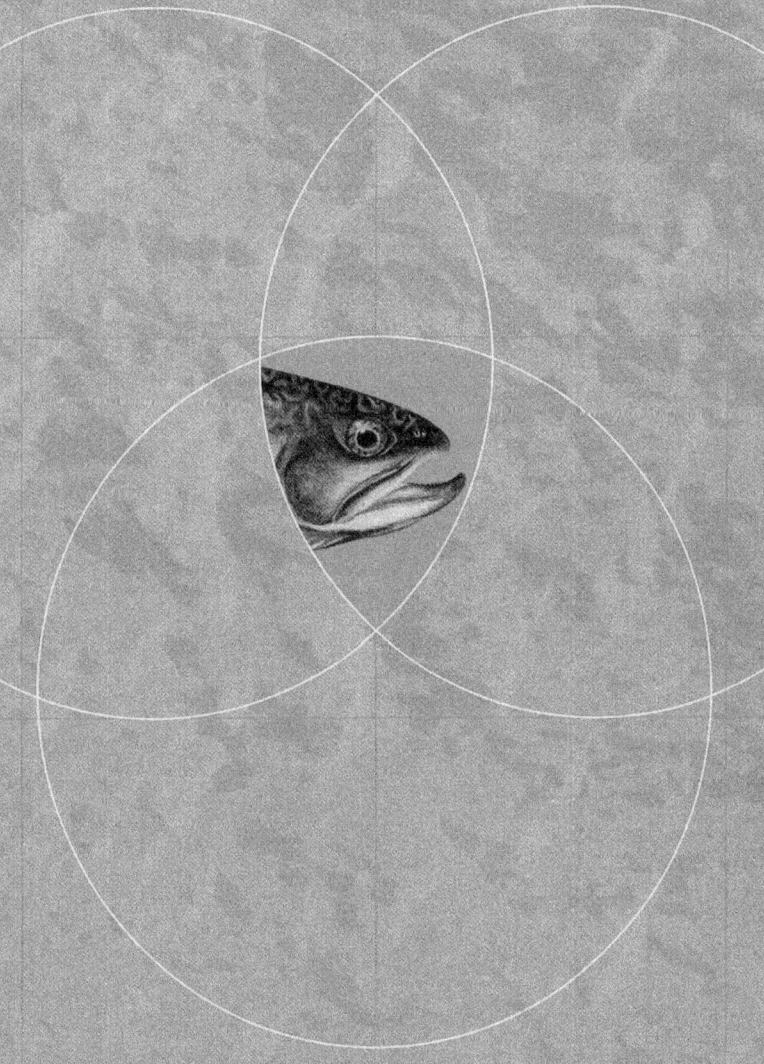

A SPECIAL REPORT BY THE
SPORT FISHING AND BOATING
PARTNERSHIP COUNCIL JANUARY 2002

Illustration: USFWS, Tim Knepp

CONTENTS

Sport Fishing and Boating Partnership Council (SFBPC)   2

SFBPC Members   3

SFBPC Fisheries Strategic Plan Steering Committee   4
Membership and Representation

Executive Summary   7

Fisheries Program Facilities Map   10

Introduction   12

Issues and Recommendations   16

THE SPORT FISHING AND BOATING PARTNERSHIP COUNCIL (SFBPC) serves as a unique adviser to the Secretary of the Interior and the Director of the U.S. Fish and Wildlife Service. The SFBPC, formed in January 1993, represents the interests of the public and private sectors of the sport fishing and boating communities and is organized to enhance partnerships among industry, constituency groups and government.

The SFBPC is chartered under the Federal Advisory Committee Act. Its membership of up to 18 people includes the director of the Fish and Wildlife Service and the president of the International Association of Fish and Wildlife Agencies, who both serve in ex officio capacities. Other SFBPC members are directors from state agencies responsible for managing recreational fish and wildlife resources and individuals who represent the interests of saltwater and freshwater recreational fishing, recreational boating, the recreational fishing and boating industries, recreational fisheries resource conservation, aquatic resource outreach and education, and tourism.

More information about the SFBPC can be found on the Internet at http://sfbpc.fws.gov or by contacting the SFBPC's offices at 703/358 1711.

SPORT FISHING AND BOATING PARTNERSHIP COUNCIL (SFBPC) MEMBERS

INTERIM COUNCIL CHAIR
William Taylor
Chairman
Department of Fisheries and Wildlife
Michigan State University

James Anderson
Executive Director
Northwest Indian Fisheries Commission

Tom Bedell
Chairman and Chief Executive Officer
Pure Fishing

Allan Egbert
Executive Director
Florida Fish and Wildlife
Conservation Commission

Doug Hansen
Director
Division of Wildlife
South Dakota Department of
Game, Fish and Parks

Paul Hansen
Executive Director
Izaak Walton League of America

Charles Harter III
Board of Directors
Coastal Conservation Association

Mike Hough
Past President
States Organization for Boating Access

Jim Kalkofen
Executive Director
Professional Walleye Trail

Barbara Knuth
Professor
Natural Resource Policy and
Management
Cornell University

Ryck Lydecker
Associate Director for State Affairs
BOAT/U.S.

Robert McDowell (ex officio)
President
International Association of Fish
and Wildlife Agencies
Director
New Jersey Division of Fish,
Game and Wildlife

Eddie Smith
Chairman and Chief Executive Officer
Grady-White Boats Inc.

Carl Wilgus
Administrator
Division of Tourism
Idaho Department of Commerce

Steve Williams (ex officio)
Director
U.S. Fish and Wildlife Service

SFBPC FISHERIES PROGRAM STRATEGIC PLAN STEERING COMMITTEE

MEMBERSHIP AND REPRESENTATION

The Fisheries Program Strategic Plan Steering Committee was assembled by the Fisheries Issues Committee of the Sport Fishing and Boating Partnership Council (SFBPC) in August 2001.

Each person on the steering committee served in his or her capacity as an individual fisheries professional. It is important to note that these individuals have served the fisheries community for a number of years and have represented many fisheries interest groups during their careers. Their breadth and depth of knowledge of a diverse array of fisheries management issues and constituents' perspectives were extremely beneficial to this project.

The following list contains the name of each steering committee participant, accompanied by the name of the participant's employer or the interest group with which the participant is affiliated. The listing of these organizations does not imply endorsement of this report by these groups. Rather, these organizations are listed to provide context for the report by illustrating the diversity of experience and philosophies that came into play during the report's creation. It should be noted that the organizations on this list recognized the importance of this report by essentially donating the time each steering committee member invested in this process.

SFBPC FISHERIES PROGRAM STRATEGIC PLAN STEERING COMMITTEE MEMBERS

James Anderson
Executive Director
Northwest Indian Fisheries Commission

Robert Batky
Chief
Division of Fish Hatcheries
U.S. Fish and Wildlife Service

Hannibal Bolton
Chief
Division of Fish and Wildlife Management
and Habitat Restoration
U.S. Fish and Wildlife Service

Daniel Diggs
Assistant Regional Director, Fisheries
Region 1
U.S. Fish and Wildlife Service

Jaime Geiger
Assistant Regional Director, Fisheries
Region 5
U.S. Fish and Wildlife Service

Mary Gessner
Assistant Regional Director, Fisheries
Region 6
U.S. Fish and Wildlife Service

Doug Hansen
Director
Division of Wildlife
South Dakota Department of Game,
Fish and Parks

Kelly Hepler
Director
Division of Sport Fish
Alaska Department of Fish and Game

Doug Inkley
Senior Science Advisor
Office of the President
National Wildlife Federation

Gary Isbell
Executive Administrator for
Fish Management
Division of Wildlife
Ohio Department of Natural Resources

Gerry Jackson
Assistant Regional Director, Fisheries
Region 3
U.S. Fish and Wildlife Service

Linda Kelsey
Assistant Regional Director, Fisheries
Region 4
U.S. Fish and Wildlife Service

John Kimball
Director
Division of Wildlife Resources
Utah State Department of Natural
Resources

Robin Knox
Sportfish Program Manager
Colorado Division of Wildlife

Jeff Koenings
Director
Washington Department of
Fish and Wildlife

Jim Kurth
Chief
Division of Refuges
U.S. Fish and Wildlife Service

Ron Lukens
Assistant Director
Gulf States Marine Fisheries Commission

Jim Martin
Conservation Director
Pure Fishing

Bob Miles
Resource Director
International Association of
Fish and Wildlife Agencies

Frederic Miller
Board of Directors
Coastal Conservation Association

Phil Million
Chief
Conservation Partnerships Liaison
Division
U.S. Fish and Wildlife Service

Christine Moffitt
University of Idaho
Representative of the American
Fisheries Society

Jim Mosher
Conservation Director
Izaak Walton League of America

Steve Moyer
Vice President of Conservation Programs
Trout Unlimited

Gary Myers
Executive Director
Tennessee Wildlife Resources Agency

Norville Prosser
Vice President
American Sportfishing Association

Jim Range
Representative
American Fly Fishing Trade Association

Stephen Rideout
Director
Silvio Conte Anadromous Fish
Research Center
U.S. Geological Survey

Don Sampson
Executive Director
Columbia River Inter-Tribal Fish
Commission

Cathy Short
Assistant Director
Fisheries and Habitat Conservation
U.S. Fish and Wildlife Service

Bruce Shupp
National Conservation Director
Bass Anglers Sportsman Society (B.A.S.S.)

LaVerne Smith
Assistant Regional Director, Fisheries
Region 7
U.S. Fish and Wildlife Service

Doug Stang
Chief
Bureau of Fisheries
New York State Department of
Environmental Conservation

Lynn Starnes
Assistant Regional Director, Fisheries
Region 2
U.S. Fish and Wildlife Service

Norman Stucky
Fisheries Division Administrator
Missouri Department of Conservation

Whitney Tilt
Director of Conservation
National Fish and Wildlife Foundation

Jim Zorn
Policy Analyst
Great Lakes Indian Fish and Wildlife
Commission

PROJECT MANAGER
John Rogers
Management Systems International

MEETING FACILITATOR
John Mundinger
Consulting for Creative Solutions

FISHERIES PROGRAM STAFF
Mike Oetker
U.S. Fish and Wildlife Service

SFBPC COORDINATOR
Laury Parramore
U.S. Fish and Wildlife Service

EXECUTIVE SUMMARY

For more than 100 years, the U. S. Fish and Wildlife Service (FWS) and its predecessors have played a vital role in the conservation and management of this nation's fisheries and aquatic resources. The FWS Fisheries Program is uniquely positioned to reach across state and international boundaries to coordinate major fisheries management and conservation initiatives. Unfortunately, a lack of clarity in its fisheries-related responsibilities, coupled with a shortage of funds and differing expectations from its diverse stakeholders, erode support for the Fisheries Program. The program must be strategically redefined to meet the fisheries conservation needs of a new century in a manner that can be supported by the Office of Management and Budget, Congress and other relevant stakeholders. To that end, the FWS asked the Sport Fishing Boating Partnership Council (SFBPC) to gather input from a broad array of stakeholders, including the states, tribes and other organizations. This report provides the consensus recommendations from that group.

Photo: USFWS

The report offers 22 recommendations that together provide a new sense of direction for the Fisheries Program. The recommendations are organized around six major topic areas:

Aquatic Species Conservation and Management

Public Use

Cooperation with Native American Tribal Nations

Leadership in Aquatic Science and Technology

Aquatic Habitat Conservation and Management

National Aquatic Habitat Plan

These recommendations build on an earlier SFBPC report, "Saving a System in Peril: A Special Report on the National Fish Hatchery System." Only through the thoughtful implementation of these joint recommendations in partnership with the full community of stakeholders will the Fisheries Program return to its position of leadership. Such leadership is essential to the health of our nation's fisheries resources.

Photo: ©Dave Cross

KEY MESSAGES CONTAINED IN THE REPORT ARE:

☐ America's fisheries and the aquatic habitats that support them are in crisis, and the FWS' ability to fulfill its aquatic conservation mission has been weakened.

☐ The FWS and its Fisheries Program must be accountable to their partners and must improve communications with them.

☐ The FWS must involve its stakeholders if it considers major alterations to its Fisheries Program.

☐ When properly supported, the Fisheries Program can be a uniquely important agent for native species conservation across the American landscape.

☐ The Fisheries Program should fulfill a leadership role in combating aquatic nuisance species.

☐ Recreational angling is important to the American public, and the FWS should re-emphasize and institutionalize support for this activity.

☐ The Secretary of the Interior and the Fish and Wildlife Service Director must work with Congress to clarify federal agency responsibilities for mitigating for the loss of fisheries resulting from federal water projects. Costs of mitigation must be recovered from sponsors of federal water projects.

☐ A major opportunity for aquatic resource conservation exists through cooperative work with tribes. The FWS should support and assist tribes in their management of aquatic resources as they exercise their sovereign prerogatives in conserving, enhancing, utilizing and managing their fishery resources and supporting habitats.

☐ The link between fisheries research and the management needs of the FWS and its partners was broken in 1993 when FWS research assets were assigned to another agency. These assets should be returned to the FWS.

☐ The Fisheries Program should be elevated within the FWS in the conservation and management of aquatic habitats.

The report also advances a major initiative to help resolve the major crisis facing fisheries in the United States — massive habitat loss and degradation. The initiative asks the FWS to assume a leadership role in convening a wide array of interests to begin the process of developing a National Aquatic Habitat Plan (NAHP). This could become the aquatic analog of the North American Waterfowl Management Plan, a science-based, landscape-scale, partnership-driven model for habitat conservation.

The steering committee believes that if the recommendations presented in this report are implemented, the FWS Fisheries Program can again become a full and committed partner in conserving America's fisheries.

Photo: USFWS

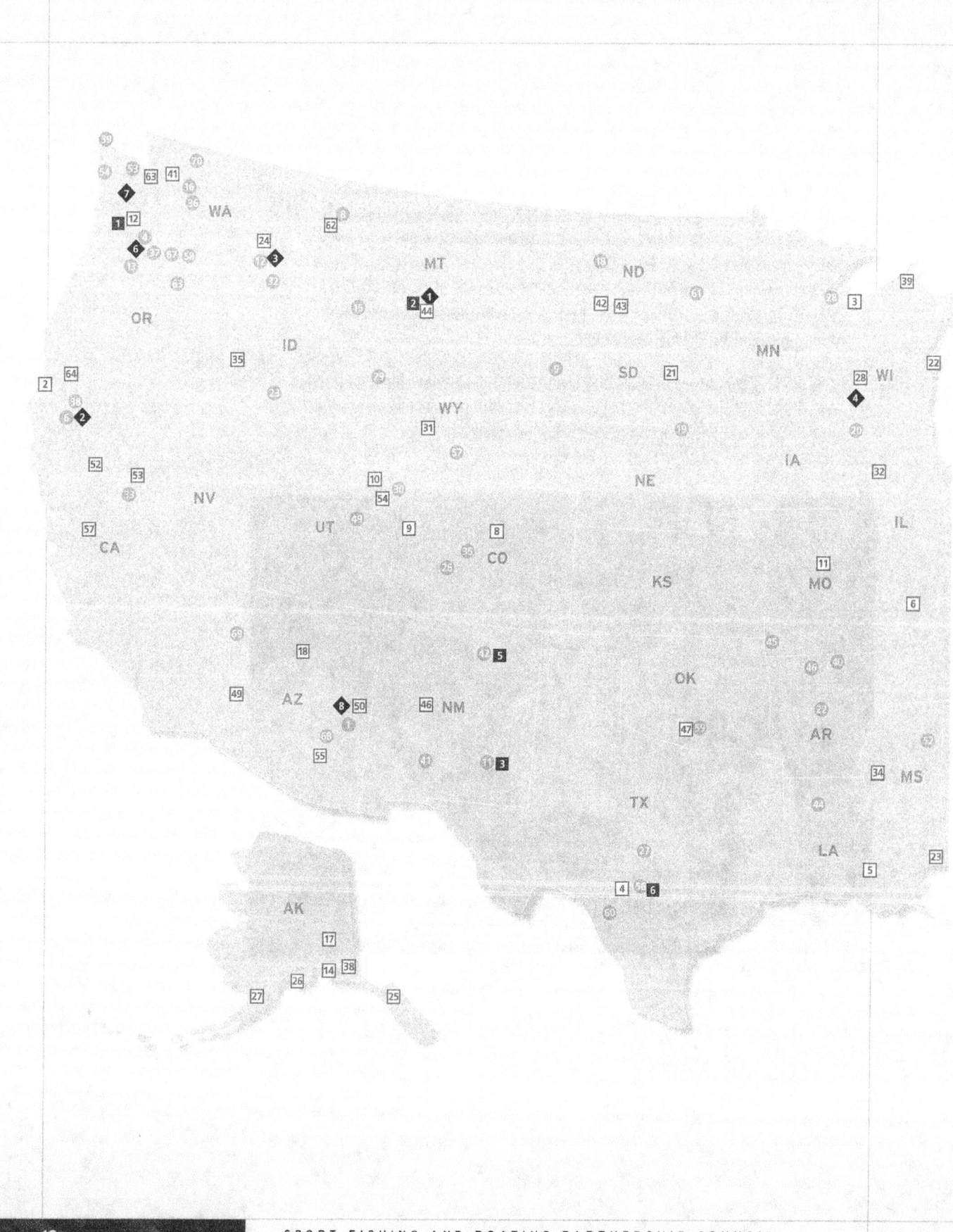

SPORT FISHING AND BOATING PARTNERSHIP COUNCIL

FISHERIES PROGRAM FACILITIES MAP

39 Makah, WA
40 *Mammoth Spring, AR*
41 Mescalero, NM
42 Mora, NM
43 Nashua, NH
44 Natchitoches, LA
45 Neosho, MO
46 Norfork, AR
47 North Attleboro, MA
48 Orangeburg, SC
49 Ouray, UT
50 Pendills Creek, MI
51 Pittsford, VT
52 Private John Allen, MS
53 Quilcene, WA
54 Quinault, WA
55 Richard Cronin NSS, MA
56 San Marcos, TX
57 Saratoga, WY
58 Spring Creek, WA
59 Tishomingo, OK
60 Uvalde, TX
61 Valley City, ND
62 Warm Springs, GA
63 Warm Springs, OR
64 Welaka, FL
65 White River, VT
66 White Sulphur Springs, WV
67 Willard, WA
68 Williams Creek, AZ
69 Willow Beach, AZ
70 Winthrop, WA
71 Wolf Creek, KY

7 Central New England, NH
8 Colorado, CO
9 Colorado River, CO
10 Colorado River, UT
11 Columbia, MO
12 Columbia River, WA
13 Connecticut River, MA
14 Conservation Genetics Lab, AK
15 *Delaware River, PA*
16 Edenton, NC
17 Fairbanks, AK
18 Flagstaff, AZ
19 Gloucester Point, VA
20 Great Lakes, MI
21 Great Plains, SD
22 Green Bay, WI
23 Gulf Coast, MS
24 Idaho, ID
25 Juneau, AK
26 Kenai, AK
27 King Salmon, AK
28 La Crosse, WI
29 Laconia, NH
30 Lake Champlain, VT
31 Lander, WY
32 Large Rivers, IL (vacant)
33 Lower Great Lakes, NY
34 Lower Mississippi River, MS
35 Lower Snake River Compensation Plan, ID
36 Ludington Biological Station, MI
37 Maine, ME
38 Marine Mammals Management, AK
39 Marquette Biological Station, MI
40 Maryland, MD
41 Mid Columbia River, WA
42 Missouri River, ND
43 Missouri River, ND
44 Montana, MT
45 Moorehead City, NC
46 New Mexico, NM
47 Oklahoma, OK
48 Panama City, FL
49 Parker, AZ
50 Pine Top, AZ
51 Raleigh, NC
52 Red Bluff, CA
53 Reno, NV
54 Roosevelt, UT
55 San Carlos, AZ
56 Sandusky, OH (vacant)
57 Stockton, CA
58 Sunderland, MA
59 Susquehanna River, PA
60 Virginia, VA
61 Wadmalaw Island, SC
62 Western Montana, MT
63 Western Washington, WA
64 Yreka, CA

* Names for offices vary

● NATIONAL FISH HATCHERIES

1 Alchesay, AZ
2 Allegheny, PA
3 Bears Bluff, SC
4 Carson, WA
5 Chattahoochee Forest, GA
6 Coleman, CA
7 Craig Brook, ME
8 Creston, MT
9 DC Booth Historic, SD
10 Dale Hollow, TN
11 Dexter, NM
12 Dworshak, ID
13 Eagle Creek, OR
14 Edenton, NC
15 Ennis, MT
16 Entiat, WA
17 Erwin, TN
18 Garrison Dam, ND
19 Gavins Point, SD
20 Genoa, WI
21 Green Lake, ME
22 Greers Ferry, AR
23 Hagerman, ID
24 Harrison Lake, VA
25 Hiawatha Forest, MI
26 Hotchkiss, CO
27 Inks Dam, TX
28 Iron River, WI
29 Jackson, WY
30 Jones Hole, UT
31 Jordan River, MI
32 Kooskia, ID
33 Lahontan, NV
34 Lamar, PA
35 Leadville, CO
36 Leavenworth, WA
37 Little White Salmon, WA
38 Livingston Stone, CA

■ FISH TECHNOLOGY CENTERS

1 Abernathy, WA
2 Bozeman, MT
3 Dexter, NM
4 Lamar, PA
5 Mora, NM
6 San Marcos, TX
7 Warm Springs, GA

◆ FISH HEALTH CENTERS

1 Bozeman, MT
2 California-NevadaC, CA
3 Idaho, ID
4 La Crosse, WI
5 Lamar, PA
6 Lower Columbia River, WA
7 Olympia, WA
8 Pinetop, AZ
9 Warm Springs, GA

□ FISHERY RESOURCES OFFICES ●

1 Alpena, MI
2 Arcata, CA
3 Ashland, WI
4 Austin, TX
5 Baton Rouge, LA
6 Carterville, IL

INTRODUCTION

The need for renewed effort to conserve the nation's aquatic resources is urgent. The fisheries and natural resources professionals comprising this steering committee — state, federal, tribal, industry and conservation groups alike — all believe the nation's fisheries resources and the aquatic habitats that support them are in crisis. The federal program with the lead responsibility for aquatic resource conservation also faces a crisis. The U.S. Fish and Wildlife Service (FWS) and its Fisheries Program must reaffirm that aquatic resource conservation is central to its mission and must directly support this mission with a commitment to working with states, tribes and other stakeholders. The recommendations of this report are consistent with the Department of the Interior's strategic planning effort, which focuses on conservation through consultation, cooperation and communication.

THE PURPOSE OF THIS REPORT IS TWO-FOLD:

☐ Provide recommendations to the FWS as it develops a positioning document that addresses issues to be covered in a strategic plan for its Fisheries Program.

☐ Provide a call to action to energize natural resource professionals, policymakers and the public to plan and create a national partnership to reverse the tide of destruction threatening our nation's fishery and aquatic resources.

The timing is urgent. Although fisheries management efforts have made some notable strides, fish and aquatic resources continue to suffer from incremental habitat loss, invasive species and nonpoint pollution. Success stories such as the recovery of Atlantic striped bass and Apache trout give us hope and illustrate the value of cooperative approaches. Nevertheless, the declines of a wide range of species — from Atlantic and Pacific salmon and American eel to robust redhorse and paddlefish — demonstrate current resource challenges.

Today, on-the-ground fisheries conservation is carried out across the United States by a mix of federal, state, municipal, tribal and private interests. This steering committee views the FWS Fisheries Program — with its 64 Fishery Resources Offices, 71 National Fish Hatcheries, seven Fish Technology Centers and nine Fish Health Centers — as an integral component of this management mix.

However, the Fisheries Program has declined steadily during the last decade. Increased pressure on fisheries resources, a lack of financial resources, and criticism of hatcheries for past practices have led to confusion about the Fisheries Program's primary objectives. This lack of clarity, coupled with insufficient communication with stakeholders, have led to an erosion of congressional and public support for FWS fisheries activities. This lack of support is evident in the program's funding, which has remained relatively flat during the 1990s at a time when other FWS activities received significant increases. Under such budget constraints, attention to restoring native species and threatened and endangered species has come at the expense of other important management areas such as interjurisdictional fisheries. An abundance of authorities but few clear, program-specific mandates has created problems with program focus. Finally, real and perceived changes in program emphasis during the last few years have weakened support from a once-strong recreational fishing constituency, states, tribes and other important stakeholders.

This steering committee presents the following 22 recommendations to the FWS with the belief that their adoption will serve to re-establish the "fish" in the U.S. Fish and Wildlife Service. The recommendations also provide direction to the agency in developing a new strategic plan for the Fisheries Program and its critically important role in reaching across state and international boundaries to coordinate major fisheries management and conservation initiatives, provide key technical support for partners, and serve as a national leader in issues such as aquatic nuisance species.

The steering committee believes the recommendations presented in this report provide an action plan that can be implemented expeditiously by the FWS, Congress and stakeholders. The consensus recommendations presented in this report are intended to assist the Fisheries Program to reposition itself as a federal leader in addressing the critical aquatic resource conservation issues facing this country.

This report builds on recommendations presented in the September 2000 SFBPC report "Saving A System In Peril," which focuses on the National Fish Hatchery System, a single element of the FWS Fisheries Program. The report identified a need for a new, collaboratively developed national strategy for the Fisheries Program. In addition, the FWS was charged by the Office of Management and Budget (OMB) and Congress to develop a new fisheries strategic plan. To that end, the FWS requested that the SFBPC, in close coordination with states, tribes and other stakeholders, facilitate a process to provide to the new FWS Director and to the Department of the Interior recommendations on developing a strategic plan.

The product of five formal meetings conducted from September 2001 to January 2002, this report is the culmination of thousands of hours donated by the stakeholder groups identified in the steering committee's membership. The report and its recommendations represent the consensus of this diverse group of stakeholders.

The report's recommendations are organized around six themes:

Aquatic Species Conservation and Management

Public Use

Cooperation with Native American Tribal Nations

Leadership in Aquatic Science and Technology

Aquatic Habitat Conservation and Management

National Aquatic Habitat Plan

These recommendations provide a blueprint from which the FWS can develop a strategic plan for the Fisheries Program. If they are addressed appropriately, the resulting plan will enjoy widespread stakeholder support and begin to repair damaged relationships with stakeholders.

Illustration: USFWS, Tim Knepp

Funding and priorities are important considerations in the development of a new strategic plan for the Fisheries Program. For the FWS to be an effective partner in fisheries conservation, it must carry out and maintain an integrated, well-balanced program. In its earlier report, "Saving a System in Peril," the SFBPC spoke to the importance of a strong, science-based hatchery activity within the FWS. This report reiterates that need and further addresses the role of the FWS in other aspects of fisheries conservation — habitat, mitigation for federal actions that have negatively affected the fisheries resource, species conservation where there is a federal nexus, and the overarching responsibility to lead in the development and application of sound science to fisheries conservation and management. All of these are of highest priority and must be maintained.

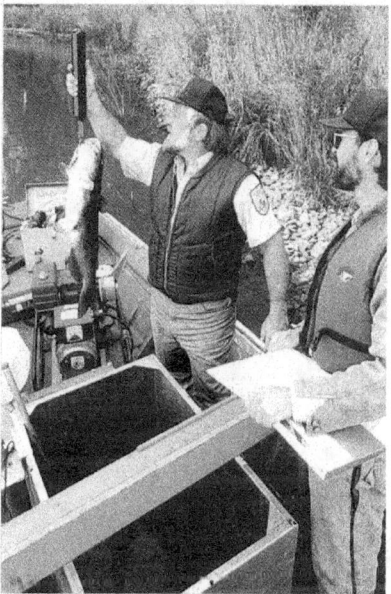

Photo: USFWS

This report strongly recommends that the FWS and the Department of the Interior aggressively pursue reimbursement for fishery mitigation activities. As this reimbursement is received and cost-savings are effected in other fishery activities, it is important to retain the savings within the Fisheries Program. A zero-sum gain is not acceptable. At the same time, the steering committee recognizes that past funding decisions by the FWS, OMB and Congress placed the FWS and its Fisheries Program in a position where it cannot continue to do all that it has and all that is expected of it. Consequently, the FWS may be forced to reduce its Fisheries Program in the near term. If this occurs, the FWS must involve its stakeholders as it considers reductions.

The steering committee further recognizes that some of the following recommendations will require new funds or redirection of funds from other activities. Sharp reductions in fisheries activities are certain to alienate virtually all constituents — states, tribes, individual anglers and others who care about aquatic resources. Such actions will reflect negatively on the FWS as a whole. Full funding for the Fisheries Program is absolutely necessary to ensure that the FWS remains a full partner in fisheries conservation and management. The aquatic resources of this country need it, and stakeholders will demand it.

ISSUES AND RECOMMENDATIONS

OPERATING PRINCIPLE

The steering committee emphasizes the critical importance of strong, two-way communications between the FWS and its partners. Too often, key management decisions affecting aquatic resources appear to have been made unilaterally by the FWS and communicated to partners only after decisions have been made, eroding partners' trust. The FWS must recognize and acknowledge its accountability to its partners. The FWS should meet regularly with its partners to jointly establish goals and objectives and also must be an active part of state and tribal processes where the FWS has an identifiable role and is asked to participate.

Recommendation

1 The FWS should involve its stakeholders prior to making any decisions that affect the Fisheries Program. The FWS should consider annual meetings at the national and regional levels to create a strong collaborative environment for aquatic resources conservation.

AQUATIC SPECIES CONSERVATION AND MANAGEMENT

INTERJURISDICTIONAL FISHERIES

Interjurisdictional fisheries are freshwater, estuarine or marine fish populations managed by two or more states, nations or tribal governments because of their geographic distribution or migratory patterns. Examples include American shad, salmon and steelhead, paddlefish, sturgeon, striped bass, redfish and sea trout.

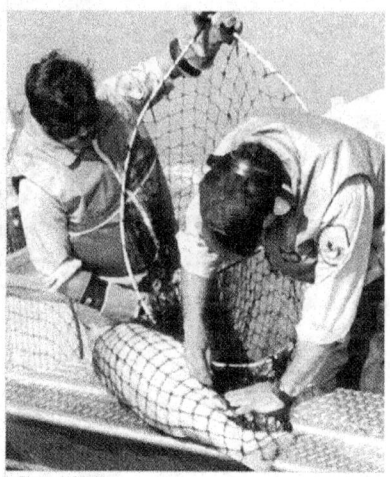

Photo: USFWS

Issue

The FWS role in interjurisdictional fisheries management, including inland and coastal environments, is poorly defined and understood. Over time, responsibility for management of interjurisdictional fisheries has been assigned by many laws, executive orders and treaties to many elements within states, tribes and the federal government. This overlap in responsibilities has led to confusion, frustration and unmet expectations on the part of the FWS and its stakeholders. Most importantly, the immensely valuable interjurisdictional fisheries resource itself has suffered.

Role

The role of the FWS is to support, facilitate and/or lead a collaborative approach to conserve interjurisdictional fisheries. The FWS has this responsibility where there is a direct mandate (statute, treaty or Executive Order). The FWS also has this responsibility where two or more states, tribes or nations manage a fishery and request support of the FWS, and a management plan is in place or is to be developed, and that plan specifies a role for the FWS.

The FWS management role is to work with partners to achieve self-sustaining fisheries. Once populations are at a self-sustaining level, the FWS role is to support state and tribal management of those fisheries by providing science and technology assistance.

Recommendations

2 The secretaries of the Interior and Commerce must develop, in conjunction with the affected states and tribes, a joint policy clarifying the interjurisdictional responsibilities of the FWS and National Marine Fisheries Service in a memorandum of understanding that is reviewed annually. The scope of this memorandum should include marine, estuarine and freshwater environments.

3 The Fisheries Program should increase efforts with interstate marine fish commissions, other interjurisdictional organizations, and their member states and tribes to develop collaborative interstate agreements for specific interjurisdictional fisheries and the habitats that support them.

Photo: USFWS

NATIVE SPECIES

Issue

The FWS Fisheries Program has made numerous contributions to the conservation of species listed under the Endangered Species Act (ESA) and species that are declining but not yet formally listed. However, in the eyes of many partners, the Fisheries Program's increased involvement in these activities in recent years has come at the expense of fulfilling its obligations for mitigation and public use. The limitations of the Fisheries Program's current budget constrain broader involvement in efforts to conserve declining native species.

Role

The FWS role in the conservation of native fish and other aquatic species is to: 1) recover ESA listed species; 2) restore species to preclude listing; 3) support efforts by states and tribes to manage aquatic species to maintain healthy and diverse populations; and 4) ensure that FWS aquaculture activities are compatible with native species conservation, fishery management plans, and programs implemented to protect public fishery resources.

The criteria governing FWS involvement in native species conservation are: 1) species listed under ESA; 2) interjurisdictional species (as defined in the previous section); 3) an agreement is in place or is to be developed with states and/or tribes and that agreement specifies a role for the FWS; 4) species occur on lands or waters managed by the FWS; or 5) the action meets tribal trust responsibilities or other statutory mandates.

Recommendations

4 The FWS Director should assign the Fisheries Program the lead role in developing and implementing recovery plans for aquatic species listed under the ESA. The FWS Endangered Species Program should budget for and adequately fund these activities.

5 The FWS Director should expand participation of the Fisheries Program in the development and implementation of comprehensive conservation plans required by the National Wildlife Refuge System Improvement Act. The FWS Refuge Program should budget for and adequately fund this participation.

6 The FWS should assist states to develop collaborative efforts to ensure the continued well-being of healthy and declining native species, so as to maintain populations and preclude a need for listing.

AQUATIC NUISANCE SPECIES

Issue

Aquatic nuisance species are second only to habitat loss and degradation as factors in the decline of native aquatic species and the loss of biodiversity. More than 4,000 plants and 2,300 non-native animals have become established in the United States. More than 200 of these are wreaking havoc in major aquatic systems. They cost more than $122 billion a year in damage to industry, municipal water supply systems, and to the environment in general. Native aquatic species are especially threatened by these invaders because of the rapid spread of new species through connected waterways. Difficulties are compounded, especially at the local or state level, because aquatic nuisance species do not recognize political boundaries and because aquatic invaders often are not detected until they have become established. More than 20 federal agencies have a role in the prevention and control of invasive species, in addition to states, tribes and other entities. Legislative authorities among and between federal and state agencies are not clear. In addition, current infrastructure and funding at the federal and state levels are insufficient to effectively combat aquatic nuisance species.

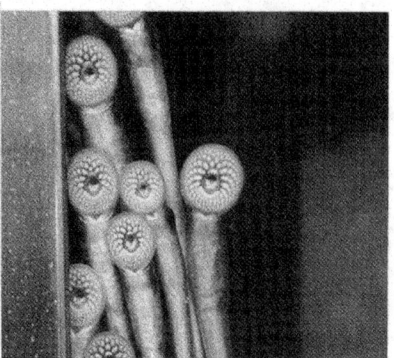
Photo: USFWS

The Nonindigenous Aquatic Nuisance Species Prevention and Control Act (NANPCA), reauthorized in 1996 as the National Invasive Species Act (NISA), provides the only permanent statutory authority for specific FWS involvement with invasive species. NISA calls for species- and vector-specific action on zebra mussels and ballast water and has broader language on prevention, detection, monitoring, research, education, control, coordination, technical assistance and the development of regional panels and state aquatic nuisance species plans. Reauthorization of NISA is scheduled for 2002.

Role

The role of the FWS in aquatic nuisance species management is to fulfill its mandated responsibilities under NISA, paying particular attention to activities that prevent the introduction and spread of aquatic nuisance species. Given the increasing threat from aquatic nuisance species and their inherent interjurisdictional nature, the FWS role and management capability must grow substantially in the coming years.

Recommendations

7 The FWS should take the lead federal role in NISA and its reauthorization.

8 The Fisheries Program should provide aquatic nuisance species technical assistance to and coordination among federal, state, tribal and other partners, as prescribed by NISA.

Photo: ©Dave Cross

PUBLIC USE

The American public benefits in many ways from the management, conservation and use of aquatic species and their habitats. For example, more than 35 million recreational anglers spent more than $37 billion, creating $108 billion in economic output in 1996. The FWS has a long tradition of providing opportunities for public use of these resources through recreational angling, stewardship projects and interpretive and education programs. The states, tribes and many other stakeholders believe the FWS should be a primary federal agency responsible for supporting public use of freshwater aquatic resources.

RECREATION

Issue

In recent years, the role of the FWS Fisheries Program in supporting public use of recreational fisheries has been eclipsed by an increased management focus on and funding for refuges, the restoration and recovery of endangered species, imperiled native species and other activities. For example, redirection of hatchery activities in some places and a perceived growing reluctance among FWS managers to publicly link their management activities with support for recreational uses such as fishing has significantly minimized the visibility of recreational angling as a recognized output of FWS fishery management activities. This, in turn, has created a perception on the part of states, tribes and other stakeholders that the FWS is on a course to abandon altogether its historic support of recreational fishing.

This diverse and increasingly alarmed constituency believes strongly that the FWS and its Fisheries Program must continue to have a significant role in supporting recreational fisheries and should do more internally and externally to articulate and carry out management activities in support of that role. The Fisheries Program can and should once again become one of the nation's leading voices in support of responsible public use of aquatic resources.

Role

The role of the FWS is to provide opportunities for angling on FWS lands, to support angling on other federally managed lands (e.g. Sikes Act), to fulfill tribal trust responsibilities, and to meet mandated mitigation responsibilities. The Fisheries Program benefits recreational fishing through interjurisdictional fisheries management, conservation of native species and their habitats, fish production and other technical support activities.

Recommendations

9 The FWS Director should implement Recommendations 12 and 13 of "Saving A System in Peril," which specifically address the use of national fish hatchery products that support recreational fishing programs:

12 FWS should recover 100 percent of costs for production, stocking and any evaluation when providing fish to support purely recreational fishing programs (e.g. not as part of mitigation or restoration). Exceptions include meeting tribal trust responsibilities, stocking on national wildlife refuges, and providing fish for small, cooperative community service projects with education and outreach benefits, such as National Fishing Week events and scouting jamborees.

13 Cooperative arrangements and exchanges between the FWS and states or tribes should continue as long as they are properly coordinated and planned. When fish are requested either by or from the FWS, the need must be defined in objectives in fishery management plans. Memoranda of agreement or other cooperative agreements between the FWS and its partners must define the general conditions for each exchange.

10 The FWS Director should instruct refuge managers to aggressively pursue ways to Increase recreational fishing opportunities on refuges, within the requirements to assure that such activities are compatible with the mission of the National Wildlife Refuge System and the purposes for which the refuge was established. This is in keeping with the National Wildlife Refuge System Improvement Act that establishes fishing as one of six priority uses of the system.

Photo: USFWS, George Gentry

Photo: ©Dave Cross

MITIGATING FOR FEDERAL WATER PROJECTS

Issue

The steering committee recognizes that a lack of funding and unclear authorities for FWS activities to mitigate for impacts of federal water projects are core problems facing the Fisheries Program and its relationship to its stakeholders. Until Congress addresses and clarifies federal agency responsibilities and roles regarding mitigation, this issue will remain a major problem.

When federal water projects were developed, the federal government committed to mitigate for impacts on recreational, commercial and tribal fisheries. Over the years, hatcheries were constructed and operated by FWS to provide fish needed to keep these promises. These hatchery programs are extremely important in supporting economically important fisheries. For example, 80 percent of Pacific Northwest salmonid fisheries are dependent upon hatcheries. Hatcheries in the southeastern United States have been shown to return $109 to $141 in economic benefit for each dollar invested for hatchery management. Mitigation activities can include habitat improvement, native species and nonnative species recovery, as well as hatchery fish production.

In many cases, the FWS is funding and conducting mitigation programs despite the lack of reimbursement from project managers and sponsors. This impairs the agency's ability to deliver other needed aquatic resource programs. In addition, FWS funding for national fish hatcheries that supply fish for mitigation has been level during the past decade and has not kept pace with inflation, thus becoming insufficient to meet the FWS mitigation role related to federal water development projects. The "Saving A System in Peril" report identifies fisheries mitigation activities as a clear FWS responsibility and asserts that the cost of mitigation should be borne by sponsors of federal projects.

Role

The role of the FWS is to provide fish and associated technical support to mitigate adverse effects from federally funded water projects as directed by statutory authority or reimbursed by project managers and sponsors.

Recommendations

11 The Secretary of the Interior and the FWS Director must work with Congress to clarify federal agency responsibilities for mitigation.

12 The Secretary of the Interior and the FWS Director must aggressively seek to recover costs of mitigation from sponsors of federal water projects. Costs for the entire range of activities associated with hatchery production and stocking for mitigation must be fully reimbursed by the party or parties responsible for the development project.

COOPERATION WITH NATIVE AMERICAN TRIBAL NATIONS

Maximum conservation of the nation's natural resources cannot be achieved without the partnership of Indian tribes. Tribes manage or influence some of the most important fishery resources and habitats on and off reservations. In addition, the federal government and the FWS have distinct and unique obligations toward Indian tribes that are based upon the trust responsibility, treaty provisions and particular statutory mandates. These obligations are recognized in the FWS Native American Policy. They differ from the federal government's responsibilities to states and other stakeholders.

Tribes, the FWS and other stakeholders have expressed certain expectations and understandings concerning tribal partnerships. They include:

☐ The FWS Fisheries Program has served and should continue to serve an important role with tribes, discharging the federal government's unique obligations to tribes and helping ensure effective natural resource protection and management.

☐ The FWS must not be paternalistic in meeting its obligations to tribes, yet it must be vigilant to ensure that its actions, programs and other partnerships do not infringe upon tribes or their fishery rights.

☐ Tribes and tribal needs/interests are not monolithic, and FWS obligations to tribes may be unique to a particular tribe or to a particular treaty. Also, tribal natural resource management programs/infrastructures vary, sometimes significantly, from tribe to tribe. This points out the need to support tribes in fully developing their natural resource management programs and to look to tribes for both leadership and expertise in protecting fishery resources and habitats.

☐ The earlier other governments and stakeholders get tribes involved in partnerships to address mutual natural resource imperatives, the greater the likelihood the partnership will succeed.

Issue

The relationship between the tribes and the federal government regarding natural resources is unique and is governed by a complex network of laws and treaties. Fishery resource needs are significant to tribes, and tribes' involvement in the decisions that affect them is equally critical. Tribes and their communities are inextricably tied to and rely upon a sustainable natural resource base to meet subsistence, commercial, ceremonial, religious and medicinal needs. It also is important to understand that funding concerns permeate virtually all tribal natural resource management issues and programs.

Aquatic nuisance species control, native species restoration, fishery habitat protection and restoration, and fish contamination are particular imperatives where support for and partnerships with tribes are critical. Many effective partnerships can be developed among the FWS, tribes, states and others to serve simultaneously each partner's objectives. These issues are addressed in the following recommendations and elsewhere in the report

Role

The role of the FWS is to support and assist tribes in their management of aquatic resources as they exercise their sovereign prerogatives in conserving, enhancing, utilizing and managing their fishery resources and supporting habitats.

Recommendations

13 The FWS Director should consult with tribes at the regional and national levels in the development of the fisheries strategic plan.

14 The Fisheries Program should provide technical assistance to tribes, as requested, and work to reduce or eliminate the costs to the tribes of these activities. Assistance in training, development of management plans, support for tribal hatcheries, fish health services and support for other facilities and activities that assist the tribes is particularly important.

15 The Fisheries Program should work with stakeholders to identify sources of funds, both public and private, that can be used to enhance tribal resource management infrastructures or for particular partnerships or initiatives involving tribes. Based on the success of the Land and Water Conservation Fund grant program allocation to tribes, explore opportunities for funding from other federal sources.

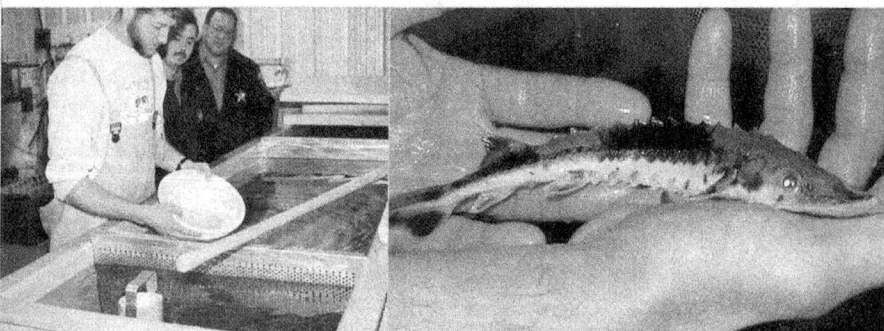

Photos: USFWS

LEADERSHIP IN SCIENCE AND TECHNOLOGY

Issue

Prior to 1993, the FWS maintained the primary science and technology capability to address fishery and aquatic resource management issues. In part, this capability consisted of the Fish Health and Fish Technology centers investigating fish culture techniques, fish health, genetics and population dynamics; research centers and laboratories examining fishway design, fish health, genetics, habitat requirements and restoration techniques; Cooperative Fish and Wildlife Research Units at colleges and universities throughout country conducting research and training tomorrow's managers; and the Fish and Wildlife Management Assistance offices, which provided fisheries outreach and technical assistance. Collectively, this internal expertise was highly valued by states, tribes and other partners for providing research in a timely and cost-effective manner.

Photo: USFWS

With the creation of the National Biological Survey in 1993 and its subsequent reorganization under the U.S. Geological Survey as the Biological Research Division (USGS-BRD), the direct connection was broken between fisheries research and the management needs of the FWS and its partners. This steering committee believes USGS-BRD is not meeting the aquatic research needs of the FWS, much less the needs of the agency's partners. This situation is only worsening.

Within FWS, the capabilities and expertise of the Fish Health and Fish Technology centers and Fisheries Resource offices are limited because of eroding Fisheries Program budgets at a time when fisheries science and technology needs are growing.

Role

The FWS role is to provide leadership in the development and application of state-of-the-art science and technology for the conservation and management of fish and other aquatic species and their habitats.

Recommendations

16 The Secretary of the Interior and Congress must restore the linkage of fisheries research and technology to management needs through changes within the USGS-BRD that allow federal, state and tribal resource professionals a primary role in determining research and training/education priorities. Selected elements from USGS-BRD should be returned to the FWS.

17 The FWS Director should provide increased funding for the Fish Technology and Fish Health centers to conduct technology development, transfer and outreach with states, tribes and others.

18 The Fisheries Program should continue its support for aquatic species drug and chemical registration/re-registration efforts (i.e. Lampricide, rotenone).

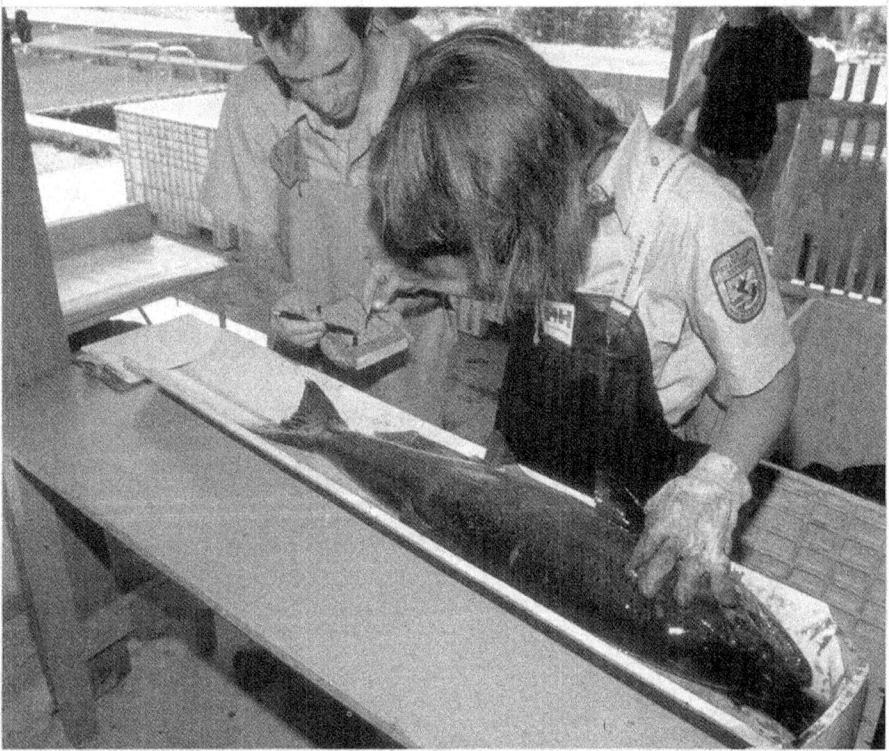

Photo: USFWS, J&K Hollingsworth

AQUATIC HABITAT CONSERVATION AND MANAGEMENT

Healthy habitats are critical to all aquatic species. Unfortunately, many aquatic habitats are threatened to the point of crisis. As a case in point, habitat alteration is the reported cause of 73 percent of fish extinctions in the last 100 years. Similarly, habitat alteration is identified as the principal factor in 63 (91 percent) of 69 fish species listed under the Endangered Species Act. The steering committee believes the Fisheries Program should be strengthened and better positioned to work with partners and stakeholders in the restoration, protection and enhancement of the coastal, estuarine and large watershed resources that are so vital to the health of so many aquatic species.

Issue

Habitat protection and restoration are central elements of the FWS mission and are fundamental to virtually everything the agency does. FWS programs are focused on the conservation, protection and enhancement of habitat through a complex array of regulatory and non-regulatory mechanisms and programs operating in conjunction with federal and state agencies, tribes and other interests. Many statutes, such as the Endangered Species Act, Migratory Bird Treaty Act, National Wildlife Refuge System Improvement Act, and Fish and Wildlife Coordination Act, provide the FWS with a mandate for habitat conservation and management. Within the FWS, different programs actively address habitat issues; however, the Fisheries Program is involved only peripherally, with the exception of the National Fish Passage Program, initiated in 1999. The steering committee recognizes that the Fisheries Program should incorporate habitat restoration and management needs into all decisions regarding fisheries restoration and management, thus becoming more habitat-based. The steering committee defines "habitat-based" as those activities that directly lead to sustainable or increased fisheries populations.

Authorities such as the Federal Power Act (Federal Energy Regulatory Commission [FERC] relicensing activities), the Fish and Wildlife Coordination Act, and Section 404 of the Clean Water Act offer the FWS opportunities to conserve critical fisheries habitat and to restore or protect fish passage on a major scale. For example, hundreds of projects are scheduled for relicensing in the near future under FERC alone. Project reauthorizations, Section 404, instream flows and other water quality and allocation issues are not managed consistently in FWS headquarters and regional offices. These management inconsistencies have lessened the agency's effectiveness in conserving aquatic habitats and species.

Photo: ©Dave Cross

The FWS is effectively using programs such as Partners for Fish and Wildlife to restore and protect habitats on private lands. To date, these programs have not met their full potential with respect to aquatic habitats. The National Fish Passage Program works effectively with partners to reconnect aquatic species with historic habitats but is under-funded in relation to the need. In many coastal areas, national wildlife refuges are major landowners whose management decisions greatly affect natural resources in their respective areas. The FWS should be more involved in implementing joint management decisions.

Role

The FWS role is to protect, restore and manage aquatic habitat on national wildlife refuges; to provide assistance and expertise in the management of aquatic habitats on other federal or tribal lands; to advise, in its regulatory role, on mitigation for federal projects; and to provide technical assistance to partners about habitat management.

Recommendations

19 The FWS Director should require the chief of the National Wildlife Refuge System to more directly engage the Fisheries Program in elevating aquatic resource conservation needs, including marine and coastal aquatic resources, in the FWS Land Acquisition Priority System. This will help ensure that consideration of these resources is institutionalized in National Wildlife Refuge System planning and management.

20 The FWS should emphasize restoration of aquatic habitats through the Fish Passage and coastal programs and cooperative efforts involving private lands partnerships such as Partners for Fish and Wildlife and the conservation provisions of the Farm Bill. The FWS should fund increased involvement of the Fisheries Program in these activities.

21 The FWS Director should expand, better focus and fund more direct involvement of the Fisheries Program in consultations on federal projects (e.g. Section 404 of the Clean Water Act, FERC relicensing activities, Fish and Wildlife Coordination Act).

Issue

The expansion of modern society has come at a heavy price to fish and other aquatic species in our nation's lakes, rivers and streams. On both coasts, once-spectacular runs of salmon are reduced to a trickle, and many species of this important and revered fish are threatened or endangered. Runoff from city streets and farm fields pollutes the water and threatens fish and people. Dams large and small alter the flow, temperature and nutrient levels of water and prevent many species, such as salmon and striped bass, from reaching their spawning grounds. Wetlands and forests give way to expanding cities and accelerating development in rural areas, and only a small fraction of waterways still are considered pristine. Invasive species are on the increase and threaten to alter the food chain, perhaps forever, in many of our watersheds.

As a result of these impacts on the landscape, native aquatic species of the country are in serious decline. Consider the following:

- More than 45 percent of U.S. endangered species live in water, and not one has been de-listed.

- Fish consumption advisories rose by 70 percent between 1993 and 1996.

- More than one-third of the nation's fish and two-thirds of the nation's mussels are listed under the Endangered Species Act.

- An estimated 2.5 million artificial barriers prevent fish passage, including 75,000 dams greater than six feet.

Photo: USFWS

The steering committee believes a partnership effort on the scale of the highly successful North American Waterfowl Management Plan (NAWMP) is needed to establish and achieve the national conservation goals necessary to rescue imperiled fisheries. A strong and viable FWS Fisheries Program, because of its national reach and unique coordination capabilities, must be at the center of this effort.

As with many natural resource issues, responsibilities for management of aquatic habitats are under the jurisdiction of a wide array of federal, state and tribal entities. Thus, management of aquatic habitats is the responsibility of all of them — or none of them. The most successful model for collaborative work to achieve large-scale habitat conservation and restoration goals across multiple jurisdictions is the NAWMP. The time is right to capitalize on the landscape-scale, partnership-driven and science-based model of the NAWMP to develop a similar effort for aquatics—the National Aquatic Habitat Plan (NAHP).

The FWS is the federal agency best positioned to work cooperatively in developing the NAHP in full partnership with other agencies having statutory authority, including the states and tribes. The steering committee envisions the plan as providing the blueprint for the conservation and management of aquatic habitats and the species dependent upon them. Modeled after the NAWMP, the plan would be organized around joint ventures, which are partnerships composed of all the communities of interest around a geographic priority (e.g. Missouri River, Columbia River Basin, Gulf Coast estuaries and wetlands, and the Great Lakes system or subunits of them, depending upon partnership decisions). The FWS initial role would be primarily as a convener and facilitator. As the plan matures, the FWS role would evolve based upon partnership decisions, available funding and legislative authorities.

The North American Wetlands Conservation Act (NAWCA) has been the vehicle at the federal level that has made much of the NAWMP project-level work possible. The steering committee additionally recommends legislation similar to the NAWCA to provide some of the resources that will be needed to make a significant improvement in the nation's aquatic habitats.

Recommendation

22 The FWS and its Fisheries Program should serve as a catalyst among states, tribes and other stakeholders to lead development of a National Aquatic Habitat Plan.

CONCLUSION

The FWS Fisheries Program cannot operate successfully in a vacuum. State, tribal, congressional and public support is the key to gaining nationwide program recognition and the requisite funding. Partners are eager to work with the FWS as it develops, communicates, implements and evaluates its new strategic plan. The time for review is past; the time for action is now.

Photo: ©Dave Cross